BIBLE PROMISES

A to Z
FOR LITTLE ME

written by:
Vanessa Duncan

BIBLE PROMISES A TO Z
Published by Daughters of Distinction LLC
Copyright ©2021 by Vanessa Duncan
Cover Design & Layout by: Ebony Richardson

All rights reserved. No portion of this book may be reproduced, stored in a retrieval system, or transmitted in any form or by any means – electronic, mechanical, digital, photocopy, recording, scanning or other – except for brief quotations in printed reviews, or articles without prior permission of the publisher.

Printed in the United States of America

Unless otherwise noted, all Scripture quotations are taken from the Holy Bible, New King James Version.

Images: all images are purchased from various vendors with rights for commerical use

This book is dedicated to

_____

Aa

Bb

He that BELIEVETH and is baptized shall be saved
Mark 16:16

Dd

DELIGHT yourself also in the Lord and He shall give you the desires of thine heart.
Psalm 37:4

Ee

Oh Lord our Lord, how EXCELLENT is your name in all the earth - Psalm 8:1

Ff

Gg

Hh

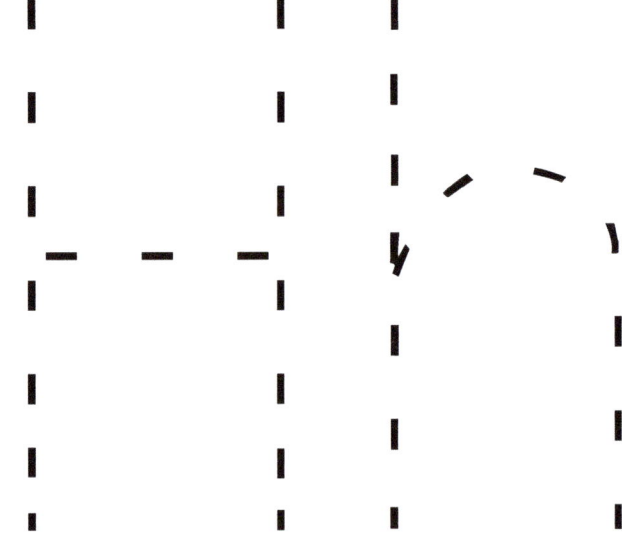

Ii

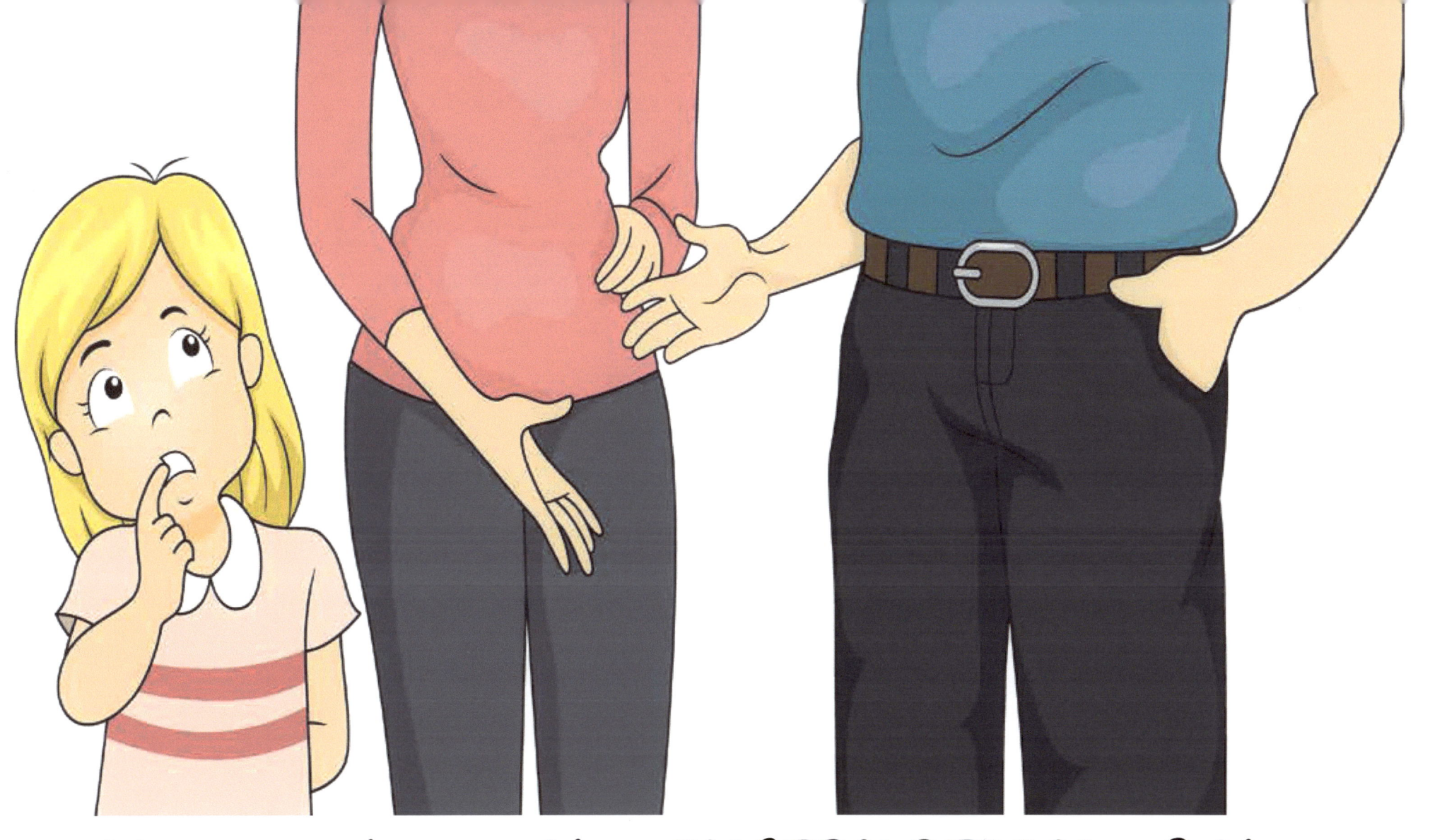

My son, hear the INSTRUCTION of thy father and forsake not the law of thy mother. —Proverbs 1:8

Jj

JESUS said to him "I
am the way, the truth,
and the life." – John 14:6

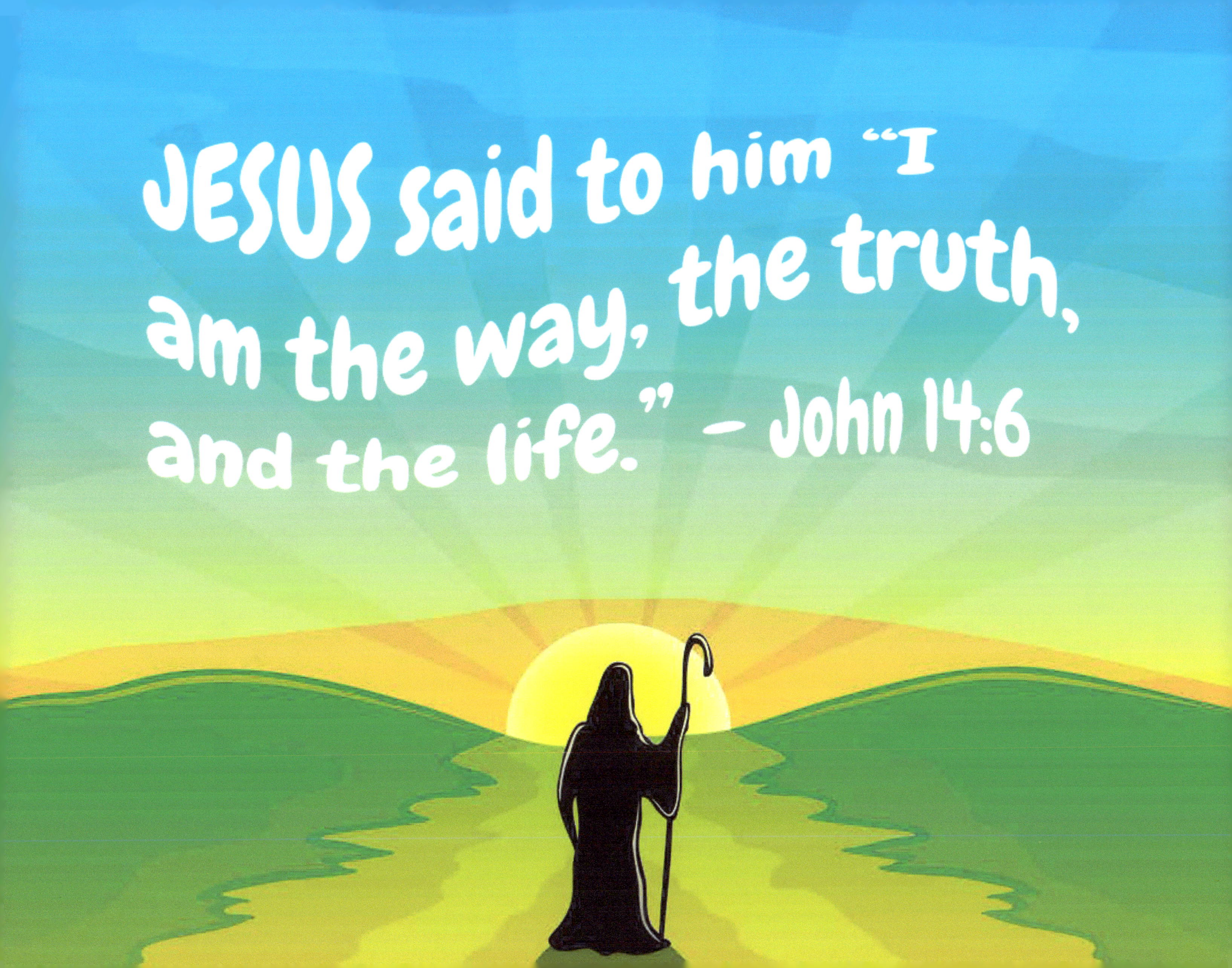

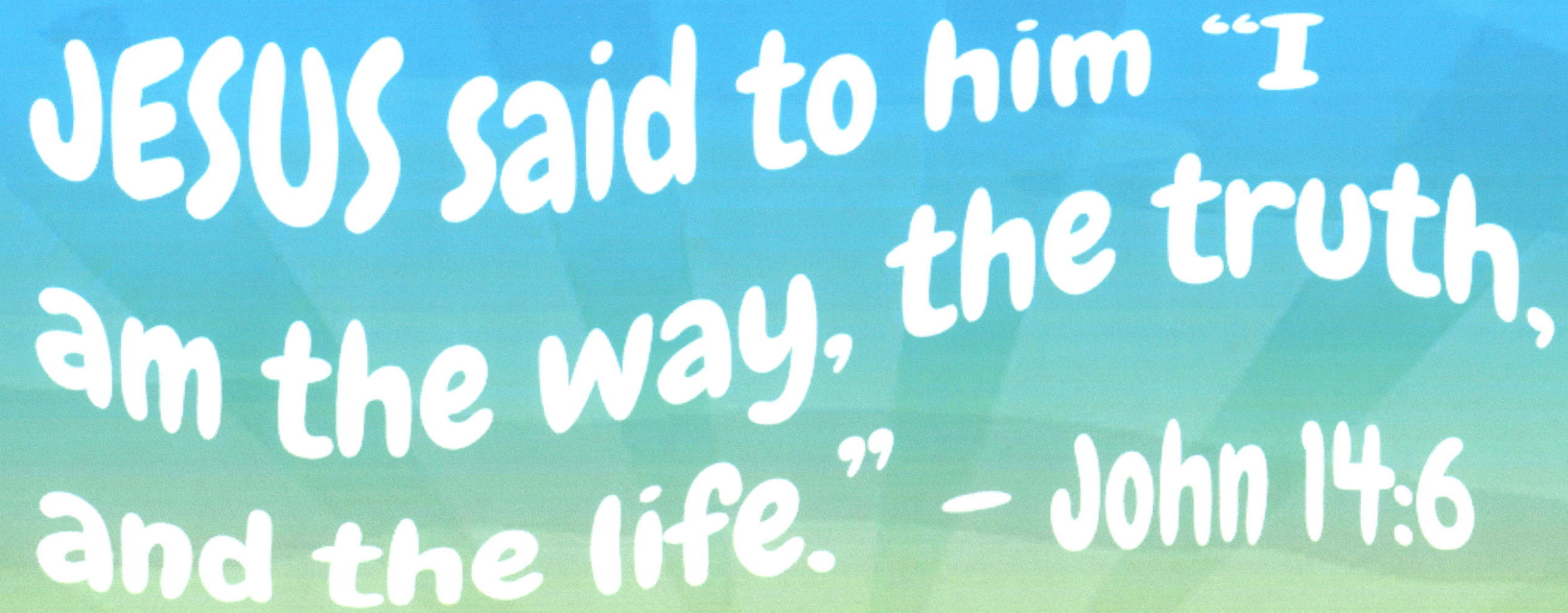

Kk

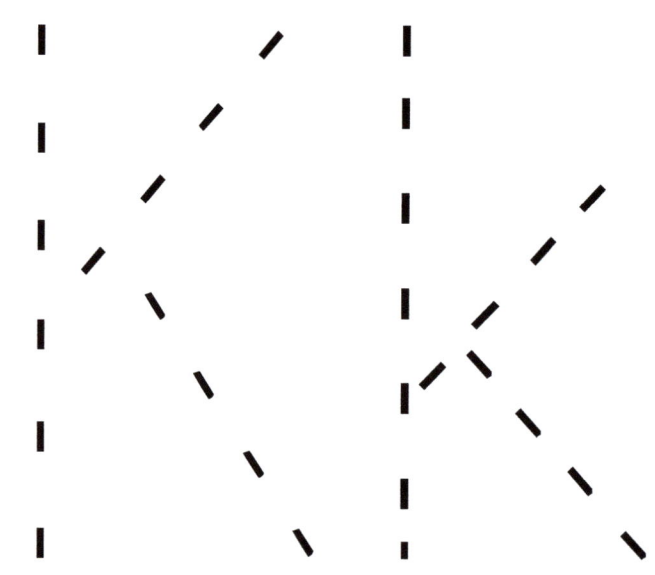

Ll

Mm

Mm

Nn

Nn

Pp

Qq

Rr

Ss

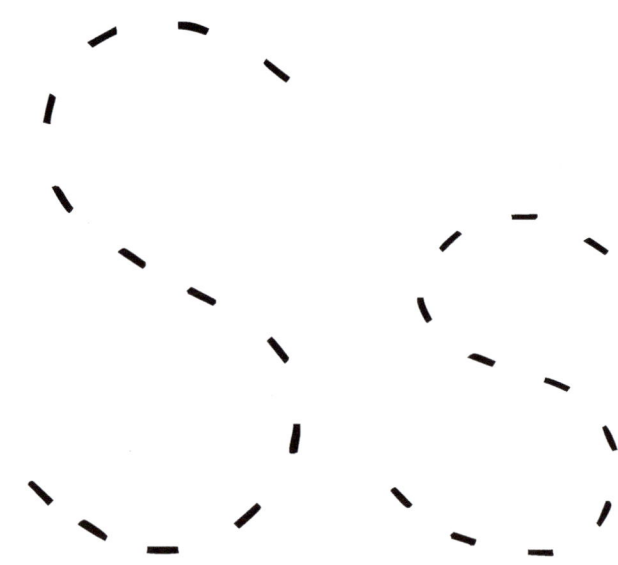

SERVE the Lord with gladness. —Philippians 4:4

Tt

T

Uu

And lean not unto your own UNDERSTANDINDING. —Proverbs 3:5

Vv

But thanks be to God, who gives us the VICTORY through our Lord Jesus Christ. – 1 Corinthians 15:57

And whatsoever ye do in **WORD** or deed, do all in the name of the Lord Jesus, giving thanks to God and the Father by him. – Colossians 3:17

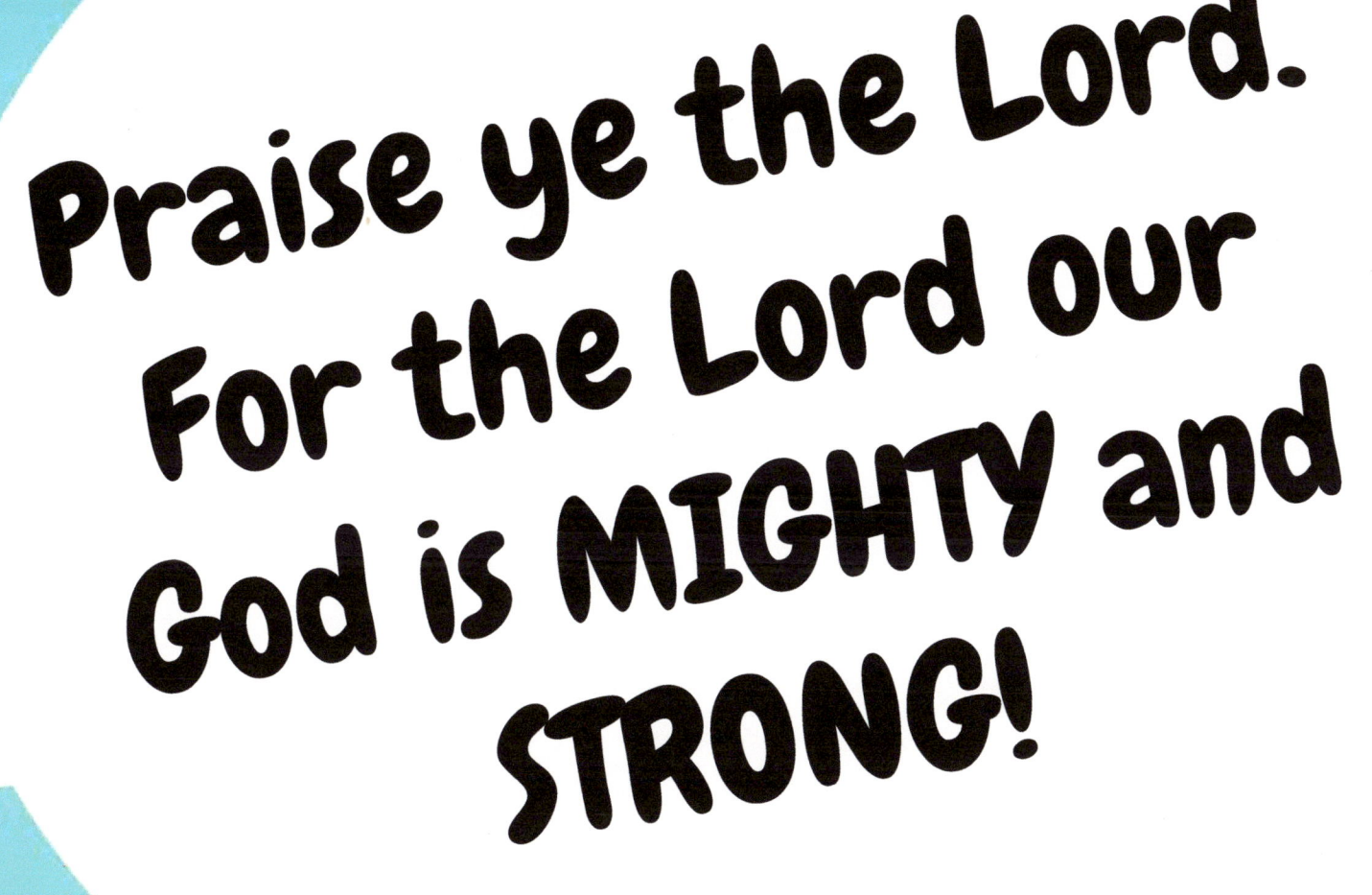

Yy

YOU shall love the Lord your God with all your heart and with all your soul and with all your mind. —Proverbs 3:5

Zz

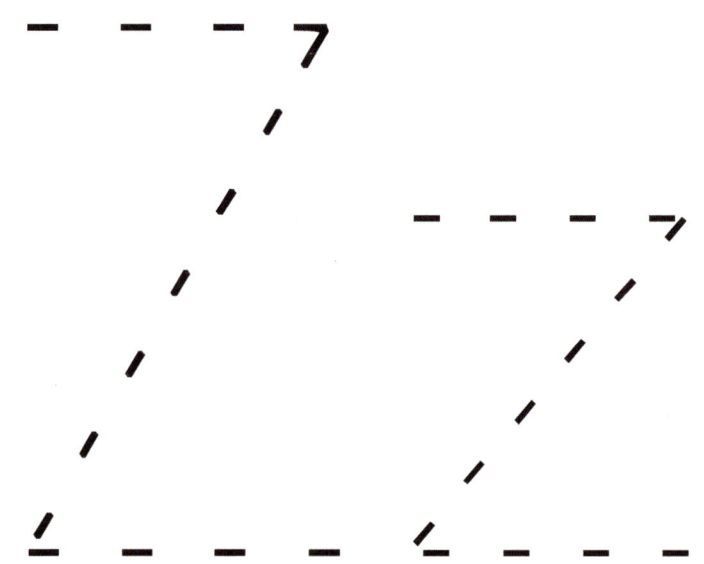

THE TEN COMMANDMENTS

I
I AM THE LORD, THY GOD; THOU SHALT HAVE NO OTHER GODS BEFORE ME

II
THOU SHALT NOT TAKE THE NAME OF THE LORD THY GOD IN VAIN

III
REMEMBER TO KEEP HOLY THE LORD'S DAY

IIII
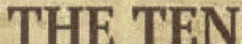 THY FATHER AND THY MOTHER

V
THOU SHALT NOT KILL

VI
THOU SHALT NOT COMMIT ADULTERY

VII
THOU SHALT NOT STEAL

VIII
THOU SHALT NOT BEAR FALSE WITNESS AGAINST THY NEIGHBOR

VIIII
THOU SHALT NOT COVET THY NEIGHBOR'S WIFE

X
THOU SHALT NOT COVET THY NEIGHBOR'S GOODS

And they are ZEALOUS of the law.. – Acts 21:20

What does it take to be used by God? More specifically, used by the Lord to care for His precious young sheep? Some of the essential qualities are in the person of Vanessa Duncan. She is a minister of the Gospel of Jesus Christ, who has served in youth ministry for over 25 years. Most recently, Vanessa is the Youth President in her local church. Secondly, one who knows how to be a mother. Vanessa is a proud mother of three sons, Travis, Tyler, Michael and one bonus son Ryan. She instilled in them to be fair, kind, and to respect others, to love God and obey Him and to work hard for what you want. She was reared with reverence for the Lord as a PK (preacher kid) to Pastor Richard and Sherleena Morris. She is an only child and has always loved little children.

In the year 2000, she left a corporate job where she worked for twelve years to develop a family daycare business. During that time, she obtained a CDA (Child Development Associate) and became a member of the National Child Care Association. Vanessa owned and operated "Love and Kindness Family Child Care" for 16 years. Other skills to care for God's precious ones emerged while operating the business.

Her mission for children is, "Train up a child the way they should go." Her vision for them is "To be safe at all times." The best way for her to do that is by teaching them the Word of God at a young age, life's basics, love, forgiveness and kindness (Deuteronomy 11:18). Teach them as much as they can absorb such as learning the alphabet, how to count, read, science, sing, use large motor skills, do arts and crafts, provide emotional support and be effective in communicating and problem solving. An additional quality to be used is to model for them, treating others with love and kindness.

In ministry, Evangelist Duncan has earned an Associate Degree in Theology, worked diligently in her local ministry as Evangelist, outreach minister, bible study teacher, intercessory and prayer warrior.

www.ingramcontent.com/pod-product-compliance
Lightning Source LLC
LaVergne TN
LVHW070908080426
835508LV00004B/283